Claire Craig & Rosemary Hurtley

REFLECTIONS OF
HOPE

FOR PEOPLE LIVING WITH DEMENTIA

CWR

CONTENTS

INTRODUCTION

I think spiritual needs do not go away. When I have fatigue I can put on my spiritual music and that inspires me and I can go into that spot through meditation or visualisation. I have kept my spiritual life going, but I do like my religious family too, which I have lost.

Agnes Houston[1]

Agnes is one of a growing number of people with dementia who have spoken about the importance of spirituality and the difference that having a faith can make when living with the condition.

This book, based around the 23rd Psalm, comprises a series of Christian reflections that can offer both people with dementia and those caring for individuals a source of encouragement and hope. Rather than providing a theological exploration of the psalm we have sought to capture its underlying message. The overwhelming sense throughout is that Jesus knows each of us by name and is the same yesterday, today and tomorrow. Whether you are living with dementia, experiencing memory problems, caring for a family member or facing other personal challenges, this psalm is a reminder that nothing, but nothing, can separate us from the love of God.

THOUGHTS ABOUT USING THE RESOURCE

Dementia is a long-term neurological condition that can impact on communication, memory and perception. Because we know that dementia can affect people in many different ways and the nature of the condition is such that it can fluctuate and change on a day to day basis, we have made the book accessible on a number of levels:

- You can focus on looking at the pictures and reflecting and talking about the images and the lines of the psalm they illustrate and in doing so meditate on God's Word.
- It is possible to read the short narratives inspired by the psalm and use these as the basis of reminiscence.
- You can also meditate on the passages in relation to what the psalm tells us about dementia and draw strength from these or use these for discussion.

We have also included a number of short exercises and activities to share with family and friends, promoting the importance of relationship and shared experience and understanding. We have sought to include a range of ideas reflecting a breadth of skills and abilities and taking into consideration the needs of individuals at very different points in their journey through dementia.

Finally, there is a prayer or a short meditation, a reflection that when we draw near to God He draws near to us.

Underpinning all of these are the RESTOR8 principles[2] which can be found in the Appendix.

Above all, our prayer is that no matter what your journey, this book will be a source of hope and encouragement.

Psalm 23

The LORD is my shepherd, I shall not be in want.
He makes me lie down in green pastures,
he leads me beside quiet waters,
he restores my soul.
He guides me in paths of righteousness
for his name's sake.
Even though I walk
through the valley of the shadow of death,
I will fear no evil,
for you are with me;
your rod and your staff,
they comfort me.
You prepare a table before me
in the presence of my enemies.
You anoint my head with oil;
my cup overflows.
Surely goodness and love will follow me
all the days of my life,
and I will dwell in the house of the LORD
forever.

The LORD is my shepherd, I shall not be in want

SHEEP AND SHEPHERDS: A REFLECTION

We live in a tiny village in Yorkshire and because we are right in the hills, when it snows, boy does it snow. One of the most moving things at this time is to see the farm workers risking life and limb to find and care for their sheep. They are out in all weathers, no matter how hard the blizzards or how deep the snow drifts. I find it so touching because it reminds me of the image of Jesus as the Good Shepherd. We've lost the meaning of what it is to be a shepherd in these present times. Shepherds were the heroes in days of old – defending their flocks from wolves and other prey – to the point where they would lay down their lives for their sheep.

David, the author of this psalm, was a shepherd and so when he says, 'the LORD is my shepherd' he knows what he is talking about. In these few lines I think he is really saying that he puts his life completely in the hands of the Lord. This requires immense trust. We might feel frightened by what is happening around us but when we trust in God, our great Shepherd, we can simply let go, safe in the knowledge that we shall not be in want. This is God's promise to us.

WHAT DOES THE PSALM TELL US ABOUT LIVING WITH DEMENTIA?

Living with dementia can feel frightening at times. It's a bit like stepping out into the great unknown and worrying whether someone will be there to catch you. People living with or caring for people with dementia have shared that one of the most difficult things about their experiences is the unpredictability of everything. Before dementia there was a sense of control over events, that everything was known. After dementia things can feel as though they are spinning out of control, into the unknown.

This psalm tells us that it is OK to feel this way. Sometimes all you can do is to focus on the now and to put your trust in God who is our Shepherd, with His promise that He will lead and guide us and provide all that we require. This trust may take time to develop but if you begin by trusting God with the small things you will find that it becomes easier to trust Him with the larger things in life.

THINGS TO DO/SHARE

God knows each of His sheep by name, He knows their needs intimately as the 'Good Shepherd'. We are all special in God's eyes. We can understand uniqueness as 'difference' but it is more than this. It is also about the special value and worth God puts on each one of us.

Activity one: supported and cared for

Look through magazines and photograph albums and identify pictures that you associate with support and being supported. Make these into a bookmark or a collage as a reminder of your support networks when times are hard.

Activity two: what makes me unique?

The **name** I like to be known by

Where I was **born** – significant places I have lived: special places I have loved

Family structure: parents, brothers and sisters, children and significant others

School days: favourite subjects, events

Important events/moments: births, deaths, marriages, family events

My job: first job, training for a profession and any significant experience in working life, awards, etc

Personality type: open and chatty or quiet and reserved, what motivates and influences my mood

Who I get on with: interest groups, friends and networks

What I believe and hold dear: life influences, significant people

Likes/dislikes: food, past times

Activities I enjoy

Key life events that have influenced me

Activity three: all about love

God understands our every need – He is our Provider and
the Creator of the world made for us to enjoy in relationship
with Him. We can go to Him in times of trouble.

Goodness and love overcome our fears.

Think of the word 'love' and write down all the words you
associate with it. Think of all the things that you do to
show love and the times when you have felt loved.

A MEDITATION AND A PRAYER

Dear Lord – living with dementia feels so difficult, so frightening at times. I feel as though I am stepping into the unknown. Lord, I ask that You will be my Shepherd, that You will guide me through this time and that I will learn to put my trust, my faith in You. I thank You for all the times that You have been there in the past. The times when You have supported me, when You have defended me. I ask You now that You would watch over me, as the Shepherd who protects His flock. Amen.

He makes me lie down in green pastures

TIME TO PAUSE: A REFLECTION

There never seems to be enough time in a day and because of this I've spent my lifetime dashing from one thing to another without a moment's rest. When my time hasn't been filled with doing, work or family, I've found myself feeling guilty. A few months ago a friend invited me to go on a walk with her. Initially I turned her down, saying that I was too busy. But then she turned up at my door saying, 'I won't take no for an answer.' I reluctantly agreed and she took me to a local beauty spot, two minutes from my home. At one point during the walk she produced a small flask of coffee, and sandwiches wrapped in greaseproof paper. We paused and found a place to sit on the grass by the path. And there we stayed, with the warmth of the sun on our faces, enjoying the fragrance of buttercups and wild grasses.

Afterwards, even though the whole walk took a very short space of time I felt completely different: relaxed and refreshed. When I read this psalm I think back to that moment. It reminds me of the importance of pausing for a moment. The psalmist says that God *makes* me lie down in green pastures, not God *invites* me to, suggesting that this is important and not an option. I believe that stopping is good and even if it is just for two minutes, it brings balance.

WHAT DOES THE PSALM TELL US ABOUT LIVING WITH DEMENTIA?

We live in a society that is supercharged and where the emphasis is on doing rather than being. Success can be equated to doing everything – having plates spinning in the air and a constant drive and pressure to do more. Dementia turns everything on its head. It can do this in a number of ways.

It reminds you of the importance of being able to stop and pause for a moment. If you are living with a diagnosis of dementia, stopping is about taking stock of what and who is important to your quality of life. Stopping is about making decisions, of deciding how you would best like to use your energy, what your priorities are.

Similarly, if you are caring for a friend or a family member who has dementia, finding moments to 'lie down' is a vital part of making sense of things, of finding quality time together and, importantly, of keeping your batteries charged and remaining well. The busier you are, the more important this time becomes.

The key is to factor in this time: first, decide how long you can do this for – two minutes, five minutes, ten minutes, half an hour, an hour? Once you have identified how long, identify when and timetable this into your day. By doing this you give yourself 'permission to stop' which makes it more likely to happen. If it doesn't work the first time, pray and keep trying and eventually you will find the necessary rhythm.

THINGS TO DO/SHARE

Activity one: five finger relaxation[3]

Five finger relaxation is a simple technique that helps you to focus your mind and slow your breathing. Sit in a comfortable position with your hands resting on your lap.

Touch your thumb to your index finger. As you do so, go back in time to when your body felt healthy fatigue, when you had just engaged in an exhilarating physical activity. You might imagine that you had just played tennis, jogged, etc.

Touch your thumb to your middle finger. As you do so, bring to mind a loving experience.

Touch your thumb to your ring finger. As you do so, think about the nicest compliment you have ever received. Try to really accept it now. By accepting it, you are showing your high regard for the person who said it. You are really paying him or her a compliment.

Touch your thumb to your little finger. As you do so, picture the most beautiful place you have ever been. Dwell there for a while.

Activity two: reminiscence

Think about what you associate with green pastures. You may think about the spring lambs and the freshness of green we enjoy in the spring. Green pastures may also conjure up memories of long summer days, school holidays, playing outside and the sense of freedom and enjoyment of the open spaces around us. Think of a green pasture or special place you like to visit.

Thinking about this place … Can you remember going for walks as a child, enjoying the flowers, the sounds of the birds or simply running around a meadow, making daisy chains, riding a bike, having a picnic, an Easter egg hunt?

What do you remember? Close your eyes and imagine a time when you were outside with the wind and sun on your face – what did you feel, what did you smell, what sounds did you hear (grasshoppers, birds, gentle breeze)? What clothes were you wearing? What did your hair look like then? Who were you with – can you describe them?

Draw a picture of something you remember and share this together or describe the event or something particular that will help to restore the memory.

Activity three: indoor gardening

Indoor gardening	Growing from seeds
Materials:	Cress or other quick growing seeds Saucer Dish Paper towel Scissors Water
Time:	5 minutes for preparation 5–10 minutes for the activity
Preparation:	Put materials needed onto the table in front of you.
Method	1. Fold the paper towel into four. 2. Cut it to fit the dish size. 3. Pour on water and soak the towel. 4. Sprinkle the seeds, close together and evenly. 5. Water daily. 6. When the seedlings grow to about $1\frac{1}{2}$ and with a pair of small leaves, they are ready to cut and eat. Put into a salad or make an egg and cress sandwich – delicious!

A MEDITATION AND A PRAYER

Dear Lord, when my life is in turmoil, in the moments I feel overwhelmed, exhausted with worry and alone, I ask that You would help me to stop, to lie down in green pastures. I pray that in these times You would fill me with a peace that passes all understanding and that You would refresh my soul and fill me with Your healing Spirit. Teach me how to rest in Your presence, how to trust in You and how to find space in a day when every moment is filled with something. Teach me how precious Your moments are. Amen.

He leads me beside quiet waters

BESIDE QUIET WATERS: A REFLECTION

For many years we've holidayed in the Lake District. One of my favourite spots is by Rydal Water. It's not as busy as some of the other lakes and I often sit there, drinking in the beautiful views. Looking across to the hills helps me to 'tune in' and reflect on God's creation. I find that the stillness of the water offers me a sense of peace. It is almost as if I am able to absorb this feeling into my body and as I do, I feel my anxieties and worries drain away.

I once told a good friend about how much I valued this experience and he bought me a picture which hangs on the wall by our front door. Just looking at that image transports me back to the still waters. If I feel that things are getting on top of me I stand in front of the picture and imagine myself back in the Lake District and as I do, I feel a wonderful sense of peace wash over me.

WHAT DOES THE PSALM TELL US ABOUT LIVING WITH DEMENTIA?

This psalm reminds us about the need to find those places that provide us with a sense of safety and of peace. Living with dementia or caring for a person with dementia can feel chaotic at times. It is during these times that seeking 'those quiet waters' can be especially important.

Of course we don't need to take quiet waters literally. It might be a place outside, somewhere in the garden; or a favourite room in the house, a particular chair, a scent or even a blanket which when we are wrapped up in it helps us to feel enveloped in love.

The message in the psalm is that God, our great Shepherd, recognises the importance of seeking places where we can experience feelings of peace, silence and tranquillity.

THINGS TO DO/SHARE

Activity one: memory board

Look through a photograph album with a friend or family member. As you do, talk about places that have a particular meaning for you, places with positive associations which bring back good memories. Make these into a memory board – a tangible reminder of where these places are and a prompt for relaxation.

Activity two: picture meditation

Take a sheet of paper and divide it into four squares.

Think of a place, somewhere that you feel safe. In the first square draw or write down words to describe colours, objects or views that come to mind in this place.

In the second square, draw or write down words to describe any sounds or aromas that you associate with this place.

In the third square draw or write down words to describe any textures.

In the final square draw or write down words that describe a positive memory you have about this place.

Activity three: ways to enjoy a breath of air

Go for a walk and enjoy the feel of the breeze, the rain or the warmth of the sun. The shepherd values all of these elements as they provide the energy we need to enable the cycle of life.

Make a visit to a country place you both enjoy and have a picnic outside. Feed the ducks if you live near a pond.

Create a vegetable patch.

Fly a kite on a windy day.

Have a warm foot spa using a bowl and some lavender oil to soak the feet. Enjoy giving each other a foot massage with simple moisturising cream/oil.

A MEDITATION AND A PRAYER

Dear Lord, help me find the quiet places where I can escape when things are hard. Lead me to quiet waters where I can experience Your peace and Your completeness. Renew my spirit and fill me with the peace that passes all understanding. I ask this in Your Son's name. Amen.

He restores my soul

RESTORATION: A REFLECTION

Keeping fit and physically active has always been important to me. For a time I used to run half marathons and the feeling this gave me was wonderful. I really prided myself on my physical fitness and prowess. I gained great value from this.

When a series of physical injuries and problems prevented me from running, my life felt in turmoil and I had to step back and re-evaluate things. I had paid so much attention to my physical self and the identity that was wrapped up in this that I realised I had completely neglected the other parts of my life, particularly my spiritual life.

While I was praying about this a great sense of peace washed over me. It was as though I had been in the middle of this great storm which had suddenly stopped and at that moment I understood this line of the psalm – 'he restores my soul'.

WHAT DOES THE PSALM TELL US ABOUT LIVING WITH DEMENTIA?

This psalm reminds us that we are not just physical and psychological beings and that our spiritual self is just as important, if not more important. The words are a wonderful testament to the fact that no matter what is happening in other areas of our lives, God can bring restoration and healing to our souls and that is a marvellous thing. We may struggle with difficult feelings that wash over us from time to time but when we rest in Jesus He makes us complete.

A person with dementia said to me the other day, 'Every day God refreshes the parts of me other things cannot reach'. We laughed together about this but I was struck by the truth in the comment. No matter how tired, how confused, how much in turmoil you are, God has the answers.

THINGS TO DO/SHARE

Activity one: resting in the moment
Spend time identifying those activities that you find restorative. Examples could include: going for a walk, petting the cat/dog, praying, having a soak in the bath, listening to music, speaking to a good friend. List as many as you can and then try to do at least one of these a day. If you find this hard, enlist the help of others to support you in doing this.

Activity two: word lists
Sometimes just thinking about a place or an activity can help you to relax. One activity I find really helpful is creating lists of words that I associate with this. They don't have to make any sense, I don't even have to write them

down – sharing them with someone else is enough. Take, for example, a list of words to describe a view:

Rugged, rocks, dark, jagged, sea, power, crashing, wind, howling, seagulls, screeching, flapping, grey, clouds, scurrying.

Or a list of words to describe a favourite place:

Cool, hushed, silent, sanctified, dark, incense, sweet, perfume, sickly, still.

Why not try and develop your own word lists around places, possessions or activities you find relaxing or restorative. Here are a number for you to begin with:

- A precious book
- A photograph
- A walk in the garden
- Sanctuary

Activity three: painting to music/prayer painting
Materials: Music, paper, art media

Description:
This activity captures the reflective quality of arts media, showing you how to listen in the 'still small places of your

heart'. Begin by playing a piece of music. Listen to the beat, its rhythm; pay attention to how it makes you feel, the images that come to mind as you listen, any memories that it evokes and, focusing on these, begin to make marks. Let your pen or pencil move across the page, responding to the music. This activity can be quite relaxing, offering much needed space, an opportunity for restoration.

It can also help you to meditate on God so, at the end of the music, pause and reflect on the process and the visual journey you have travelled. Different types of music and visual media will yield very different results, so try experimenting. Here are a few suggestions of pieces of music you might find useful:

- Handel's *Messiah*
- 'Lord of the Dance'
- Faure's *Requiem*
- 'Thine be the Glory'

You could also use Taizé or gospel music, or music with a rhythm or a drum beat. Worship songs by artists such as Matt Redman or Tim Hughes would also be effective.

MEDITATION AND A PRAYER

Lord God, You created me and You know me. You crafted my physical being, my emotional being and my spiritual being and You made me whole. I ask, Lord God, that in times of turmoil and confusion You would send Your healing Spirit to minister to my every need and restore my soul so that I may be made complete in Your love. In Your Son's name. Amen.

He guides me in
paths of righteousness
for his name's sake

FINDING YOUR WAY: A REFLECTION

I have no sense of direction – it's a standing joke in my family that I can't even find my way out of the village where we live. I can get lost at the best of times. One year, whilst on holiday in Scotland, there was a moment when I suggested we take a 'short cut'. Needless to say we were hopelessly lost for hours and saved only when I 'recognised a wall'.

Of course I am talking here about being physically lost, struggling to find my way around new and unfamiliar places, but there have also been times when my life has spun off course and I've managed to somehow 'lose my way in life'. Work has taken on more of a priority than close relationships, or I've put too much emphasis on monetary rewards or status.

David, the author of this psalm, was all too familiar with this feeling of losing his direction in life. Promoted by God from a humble shepherd to king of Israel things were going well. However, power went to his head, and he decided that he knew the direction he was going in. As a consequence he stopped listening to God and started to make some bad decisions – some *very* bad decisions.

However, in this psalm, he reminds us that no matter how 'lost' we are feeling – either physically, emotionally or spiritually – God is there and if we ask Him He will show us the way. All we have to do is to draw near to God and He will draw near to us.

WHAT DOES THE PSALM TELL US ABOUT LIVING WITH DEMENTIA?

We all have a picture of what we hope our future will be like and most people carry around a long-term plan in their head, setting out where they hope to go next. Therefore anything that disrupts this can throw our plans out and lead to feelings of confusion. Being diagnosed with any illness or long-term condition that requires us to make this adjustment can make us feel 'lost'. We thought we knew where we were going and now suddenly we have to rethink this.

At these times we need to find a new direction, come up with a new plan to help us navigate this new reality with which we are faced. To do this we need to put our trust in God and our friends and family. We need to identify what brings us meaning, and any roles we may value, and make decisions about what is important to our quality of life. For some people this might be about maintaining friendships, for others it might be about being able to take part in activities that bring pleasure, such as music or art. Agnes Houston, a person with dementia, sums up something of the new possibilities that living with dementia has offered her in the following way:

I'm not saying dementia's not serious. But I'm going to say that it's a licence in a way, a licence to be free, to be me. I think when I got the diagnosis I got permission to be more relaxed into this person and accept her.

I wanted to find out if I was artistic. Creativity's an aspect I want to explore. Being able to feel out of the box is what I'm picking up. It will happen. It's a bit like waiting on Christmas. You know it's coming, but as a child you don't know exactly when. It's a nice feeling.[4]

Dementia can be very unpredictable and we may need to do this one day at a time, identifying signposts to help us along the way. Remember, no matter how lost you may feel, that with God everything is possible.

THINGS TO DO/SHARE

Activity one: under the watchful eye of God

Remember that God is always there for us and He is watching over us. This activity can help us to think about this in a different way, using colourful yarns and natural materials.

You might like to do this alongside a friend or family member so you can watch each other's 'Eye of God' glow. You might want to do this over a period of time – as you add a new colour or you find you get tired.

EYE OF GOD – WEAVING ACTIVITY

Materials: Scraps of yarn such as wool, various colours and textures

7" (18 cm) lengths of dowel or even better, sticks or branches from a tree or 1/2" wide strips of wood (kindling wood or anything straight). You can make the vertical stick longer if you want to represent 'the cross'.

Method:
1. Mark the middle of each piece of wood with pencil.
2. To secure the pieces of wood, lash/bind pieces together with yarn by binding the end of it around the centre of the cross you have made, using your chosen colour for the 'eye', which will be larger than the outer colours.
3. Begin to wind the yarn around each branch in either a clockwise or anticlockwise direction. Turn the frame round as you wrap the wool around each cross piece and continue to wind outwards in circular direction. You will build up a diamond shape which is flat on the front and shows bound sticks on the back.
4. If you choose to work from the front (this is the smooth side) take the wool and continue to wind it round each crosspiece in a clockwise or anticlockwise direction

from the top point of the crosspiece facing you, taking it round to the side crosspiece and so on as you continue to work.

5. Change the colour when you have made the 'eye' as you continue to work outwards. To do this, tie the new colour to the old colour, securing with a knot. You can use as many colours as you like.

6. If you want, you can finish by winding tufts around each end of exposed crosspiece – then hang it on a wall!

Activity two: mapping success

Maps can be a wonderful source of stimulation and provide a perfect talking point. Choose a theme to focus on: for example, holidays, places I have lived, places I have worked, places I have worshipped in. Take a map and mark on it these places, recalling particular events or memories that you have about that place. You could also use the internet to find images of these places and use these to create a visual collage. As an extension of this find out from your local church whether there are any local pilgrimages or opportunities to go on a pilgrimage. Recently these have increased in popularity and offer an excellent way to meet people and to deepen your walk with God.

Activity three: taking a camera for a walk
Materials: throw-away camera

To begin, think of things that you enjoy about walking and some of the things you might like to photograph on your walk. Perhaps you could decide on a theme, for example choosing to take photographs of particular colours, textures, memorable views, landmarks.

Print the images and then use these to create a visual map or collage to represent the walk. You could add to this by arranging the photographs so that they tell a story of what happened.

A MEDITATION AND A PRAYER

Dear Lord, You say that You are the way, the truth and the life. During those times when I feel lost or confused I pray that You would lay out Your new paths, Your new plan before me, and that You will lead me to pastures new, safe in the knowledge that Your love is sufficient for me. Amen.

Even though I walk
through the valley of
the shadow of death,
I will fear no evil

DARK TIMES: A REFLECTION

Life can be hard. In my experience, when things go wrong it's not just one thing but a succession of things which then seem to pile up on top of each other, to the point where you feel as though you simply cannot cope. There have been a few times like this in my life when I have felt lost and frightened and incredibly alone, when I have cried out to God, saying, 'Why me? I just can't cope any more'.

The image David uses here sums up those times: 'the valley of the shadow of death'. But the image here isn't one of despair since even in these darkest of times David reminds us that we 'should fear no evil'. Yes, things might feel as though they are closing in, but God is so much bigger than death and despair. He has promised to be there and we stand strong in the reassurance that amidst everything, perfect love drives out all fear. He will never leave us. It is God's promise.

WHAT THE PSALM TELLS US ABOUT LIVING WITH DEMENTIA

The image of walking 'through the valley of the shadow of death' is a powerful one. Yet the psalmist writes that even in this very darkest of places 'I will fear no evil'. This is such an encouragement and a powerful reminder that even in those times which seem impossibly difficult, when despair pushes in from all sides, the hope we have in Jesus is greater. Not only has He gone before us but He is with us in all that we face. Imagine that, He is there with us in every situation.

The kind of trust the psalmist describes here doesn't necessarily come about overnight. You might need to take small steps, to trust God with the details before feeling confident that you can trust Him with the bigger things. The important thing to remember is that God is there no matter what. We need to focus on Him and keep moving forward.

THINGS TO DO/SHARE

Activity one: the shield of faith

One of the images used in the Bible in association with difficult or challenging times is that of the shield. In Ephesians we are told to 'take up the shield of faith' and this activity reminds us of this, inviting us to create our own shield, reflecting something of our past achievements, potential obstacles, possible resources and, finally, a motto or a word from Scripture. This exercise is a variation of the popular shield activity used in many group settings.

Draw the outline of a shield and divide it into four segments. In the first segment either write words or create images that reflect something of your strengths. In the second segment write words or create images that reflect something of the challenges that you face. In the third segment write words or create images of some of the resources upon which you can draw, and in the final segment write down a motto or a line from Scripture from which you draw strength.

Activity two: bookmark

Begin by looking through the Bible to find references to the confidence we have in God in the face of fear. Examples could include:

Perfect love drives out fear (1 John 4:18)

I sought the LORD *and he answered me; he delivered me from all my fears.* (Psalm 34:4)

'For I am the LORD, *your God, who takes hold of your right hand and says to you, Do not fear; I will help you.'* (Isaiah 41:13)

For God did not give us a spirit of timidity; but a spirit of power, of love and of self-discipline. (2 Timothy 1:7)

Materials:

A piece of thin card	Glue
A photograph	A pair of scissors
A ruler and pencil	A sheet of sticky-backed plastic

Method   1. Spend time choosing the photograph or picture that you would like to include in your design. The picture might be too large and if this is the case you will have to consider which part of it will form the bookmark. Use the pencil and ruler to mark which part of the picture you are going to use.

2. Use the scissors to cut the picture to size.

3. Choose the piece of card you will use. Place the picture onto the card to gain an idea of how big it will need to be and again use the pencil and ruler to mark this out. Make sure you leave enough space to be able to write the words of your Bible verse around the image.

4. Cut out the card using the scissors. Next glue the back of the picture and stick this firmly to the card.

5. Write the words of your Bible verse around the image.

6. To protect the picture from the print of the book you need to cover the bookmark. Measure out the size of the bookmark onto sticky-backed plastic and cut this out.

7. Peel off the backing sheet and stick the plastic to the front of the bookmark.

8. Your personalised bookmark is now completed.

Activity three: voices of reassurance

Invite friends and family to help make an audio tape of their voices reading comforting poems, with some music and words of encouragement that you can listen to.

A MEDITATION AND A PRAYER

You are an eternal God. Age does not weary You,
   nor death destroy.
New life You give us every day.
You are outside time, and we see
All round us new places, scenes and people around us,
And in every one You are there with us.
Your perfect peace flows like a stream of everlasting water
   all the way
Into the ocean of Your love. Amen.

For you are with me;
your rod and your staff,
they comfort me

SCARVES AND CROSSES: A REFLECTION

I do a fair bit of travelling with my job but if you were to ask me what my 'must-have' travel items are I would gladly substitute my computer and posh evening frock for an old shabby scarf and a tiny hand-held wooden cross.

Let me explain: the scarf, a wonderfully worn woolly with its multi-coloured stripes, belongs to my husband. I might be on the other side of the world but as soon as I wrap the scarf around me, the scent of his aftershave which is so embedded within the fabric reminds me of him. We might be thousands of miles apart but when I am wearing that scarf I feel that he is there with me and that anything is possible.

The cross: this is particularly important and I carry it everywhere in my pocket. It is small enough for me to cradle in my hand and when I hold it, no matter what the situation, it reminds me that God is nearby.

In his psalm David identifies the rod and the staff as objects which offered him comfort. These were the symbols that reminded him that God the Shepherd was in control, that he wasn't on his own.

WHAT DOES THE PSALM TELL US ABOUT LIVING WITH DEMENTIA?

I have worked alongside people with dementia and their carers for a number of years and over this time I have come to recognise the importance of objects and the value that people attach to them. Dementia might impact on a person's ability to name these at times, but many individuals have used possessions or objects to gain clues and cues to orientate themselves or even to identify who someone is. For instance, I have been variously known as 'the lady with the paintbrush' or 'the girl with the art-box'.

The psalm tells us of the power of objects and symbols, physical reminders of God's love in times of need. These symbols can bring comfort, help us to orientate ourselves and re-focus when feeling overwhelmed by the enormity of everything. We will all have objects that enable us to do this. These might relate specifically to our faith – a cross in our pocket, a small Bible. Alternatively they may be reminders of a specific person or relationship. Perhaps this psalm reminds us that when things are difficult even the best of us need a tangible reminder that we are loved, and loved unconditionally.

THINGS TO DO/SHARE

Activity one: writing around an object

Identify different objects that help you draw close to God. It is possible to find inspiration from the most unlikely of objects – a stone, a rock, a chain, an old pair of boots. All these can have resonances with themes or images within the Bible and form the basis of poetry and prose. Use these as the stimulus for creative writing or for discussion. The following suggests examples of how to do this:

When looking at an object it can be helpful to imagine that you are looking at it for the first time. What do you notice about its shape, its colour? Does it have a scent or an aroma? If you are able to, cradle it in your hands, close your eyes, ask yourself: How does it feel? Is it cool, warm, rough, smooth to touch, is this natural or man-made?

Then you can begin to probe a little deeper. What journey has it travelled, how did it come into your possession? What is the story of its creation? If it is man-made what of the person who crafted it? What was their intention as they breathed life into it? Is there an emotional attachment? Over time what has it witnessed (key historical events, change), what story does it tell?

There are so many possible objects and angles that you could write from. Once you begin you will find it difficult to stop.

For example, during a recent writing workshop in church we discovered that the following all had a story to tell:

cross	stained-glass window	candle
cassock	crucifix	confetti
chalice	bread	

Here is a poem written by a person caring for someone with dementia:

The candle speaks
My flame has shone brightly through the ages
Bringing light to all who gaze upon me
Symbol of hope
Lighting the path of those who seek
Rejected by those who skulk in the shadows,
Those who take refuge in darkness,
Fearing the truth and what the light might reveal.

Activity two: similies and metaphors – earthly descriptions for heavenly treasures

God is a God of greatness, of power, of love, of splendour. It can feel daunting at times finding words to describe all that He is. David does this beautifully in the images he creates in this psalm. The Bible is full of incredible descriptions that enable us to catch a glimpse of God and to begin to grasp His many facets. One way that it does this is by offering images that tap into our experiences and help us to make connections with these. As a result there are lots of instances where we read what God is 'like'. Here are a few examples taken from the Psalms:

The LORD is my rock
my fortress and my deliverer (Psalm 18:2)

The LORD is my light and my salvation …
The LORD is the stronghold of my life (Psalm 27:1)

Your word is a lamp to my feet
and a light for my path (Psalm 119:105)

You can also find lovely descriptions of what it is like to be a Christian:

Those who trust in the LORD are like Mount Zion, which cannot be shaken but endures for ever (Psalm 125:1)

The following exercise asks you to describe God in a similar way, to find ways of expressing how you see Him, basing your descriptions on familiar things. Try these for starters:

- God's love is like …
- God's justice is like …
- His blessings are like …

- His grace is like …
- His power is like …
- His peace is like …
- His Word is like …

When doing this think about the familiar, the everyday. Then every time you come across this object remind yourself of this exercise and of the link you make with God.

A MEDITATION AND A PRAYER

Lord Jesus, sometimes I feel so empty, so lonely and exposed. I know that You are there but You feel so distant, so far away. Dear Lord, I long to reach out and touch You, to call on You to take my hand and hold me close so that I can feel the warmth of Your love and the stillness of Your peace. Dear Father, I ask that You would enable me to find You in the ordinary, the everyday and that You would speak to me and support me through friends and family reminding me that You are with me in all I do. Amen.

Surely goodness and love
will follow me all the days
of my life, and I will dwell in the
house of the LORD for ever

COMING HOME: A REFLECTION

What an incredible image David paints here: to 'dwell in the house of the LORD for ever'. I wonder what picture this paints for you. For me it conjures up an image of coming home after a long day. People often laugh at me when I tell them that one of my favourite things during winter, when it's dark at about four o'clock, is heading back to my little house. As I round the corner, my home comes into view and I can see the glow of the lights and my spaniel up at the window looking out for me. My pace quickens and I fumble a bit to get my key out of my bag. But as soon as I step through that front door I have the loveliest feeling ever of being enveloped in warmth before being knocked over by Eddie the dog, desperate to give me a proper welcome. It is wonderful. No matter how hard the day, how difficult the journey back, in that moment all is forgotten. Sometimes, I just sit on the settee in my front room, still with my coat on, savouring the moment of being back in a place where I can simply be me.

This line of the psalm reminds me of this moment – being in a place where you feel completely safe and secure in God's goodness and love, a place of no pressure, no need and where it is enough just to be.

WHAT THE PSALM TELLS US ABOUT LIVING WITH DEMENTIA

Living with a diagnosis of dementia or caring for a person with dementia can have the effect of suddenly bringing everything in life into focus, leading us to consider or reconsider our priorities, to identify what is important, to recognise what and who it is we value. Sometimes it means that things we previously believed to be important are suddenly seen for what they are.

This psalm strikes at the heart of this. When David asks the question 'What is important in my life, what is my heart's desire?' the answer is clear – his relationship with God is paramount – to 'dwell in the house of the LORD'.

Over the years Rosemary and I have worked alongside many people with dementia and the overwhelming message that people have shared is the way that dementia has reminded them of the importance of love and of relationship. This might be about the unconditional love that Jesus has for each one of us, reflected in the love of family and friends or our love for others. This love offers security, safety, it is all-enveloping, comforting. Rosemary's mother, a person who had dementia, captured this when she said to her, 'When I am with you I am home'. Perhaps ultimately what dementia shows us is that when we put our hope in Jesus, when we focus on loving and being loved by others, then we are indeed home.

THINGS TO DO/SHARE

Activity one: a collage

Either make a collage representing the 23rd Psalm – or think about a house you remember and think about the smells, the atmosphere, the type of rooms, furnishings, how the rooms were used, which had particular significance and memory associated with each. Thank God that He is preparing somewhere magnificent, without fault or blemish, that will last forever.

Remembering the good things in your life now – do a life-scape of appreciation. You can do this in a couple of ways: either you can draw a house set out as a plan with different rooms, or using your photographs you can just imagine a house with people living in it with you who have been or still are important to you in life. You can write their names in the rooms in your imaginary mansion if you like.

The psalm talks about many others living in the mansion. There are many people whom we appreciate through our lives and this activity will bring back fond memories of those we have loved. 'Who will be living in your mansion with you?' Look at some of your family photographs and as you go through them, think of something about that person that makes them special or something you remember about them.

We all are different and varied. God is a God of variety and it is good to be reminded of others we know and love in our lives. Relationships are what life is all about. Living in a family helps us to learn about the richness of other people and how to live together. It will be interesting who we find to be our neighbours in the different rooms!

Activity two: recipe for joy

A good measure of reflection and beauty, a sprinkling of thoughtfulness, a large tablespoon of real listening and kindness; thoroughly mix with appreciation and understanding. Take a teaspoon of humour and mix with creativity and playfulness and thoroughly mix with love. Sprinkle with hope to garnish.

Now thinking of the above with your relative or friend, write up your own personal recipe for joy. Make it as lively as you wish and draw and decorate it with whatever symbols etc you like.

Enjoy this as something you can add to throughout your life and keep it as a reminder to yourself and others of your deeper needs.

Describe what things make you feel happy and deeply secure.

Activity three: developing your personal creed

A creed is a statement of belief, usually a statement of faith that expresses shared beliefs of a community. You may already be familiar with a number of different creeds, for example the Nicene Creed below. Creeds are useful because they help us to focus on what we believe and on what is important to us.

We believe in one God the Father Almighty, Maker of heaven and earth, and of all things visible and invisible.

And in one Lord Jesus Christ, the only begotten Son of God, begotten of the Father before all worlds, God of God, Light of Light, Very God of Very God, begotten, not made, being of one substance with the Father by whom all things were made; who for us men, and for our salvation, came down from heaven, and was incarnate by the Holy Spirit of the Virgin Mary, and was made man, and was crucified also for us under Pontius Pilate. He suffered and was buried, and the third day he rose again according to the Scriptures, and ascended into heaven, and sitteth on the right hand of the Father. And he shall come again with glory to judge both the quick and the dead, whose kingdom shall have no end.

And we believe in the Holy Spirit, the Lord and Giver of Life, who proceedeth from the Father and the Son,

*who with the Father and the Son together is worshipped
and glorified, who spoke by the prophets. And we
believe in one holy catholic and apostolic Church. We
acknowledge one baptism for the remission of sins. And
we look for the resurrection of the dead, and the life of
the world to come. Amen.*

This final activity invites you to do one of two things.
Either spend time with someone you trust who
understands how important your faith is to you and
create your own personal creed, focusing on your
personal beliefs; or create a poem or a list of what is
important to you, what brings you pleasure, what makes
up your quality of life. A beautiful example of this,
written by a person with dementia, can be found below.
Frame your writing and keep it somewhere safe.

*Someone who listens
Someone to talk with
Kindness and understanding
Someone to laugh with
'Me' to see 'me' a lot
I like to be liked
I like to please
I like to know what pleases you so that I can pass it on
to someone else
Doing things, loving people*

Letting them know you are thinking of them,
I like to see the light come into their face because
I have said something that really makes them happy,
… because I had so much unhappiness as a child
It is not so much about what people do but about
relationship.

Edith Brooking

A FINAL PRAYER

The Lord's Prayer
Our Father in heaven,
hallowed be Your name;
Your kingdom come;
Your will be done,
on earth as in heaven.
Give us today our daily bread.
Forgive us our sins
as we forgive those who sin against us.
Lead us not into temptation;
but deliver us from evil.
For the kingdom, the power and glory are Yours
now and forever.
Amen.

APPENDIX

USING THIS RESOURCE

Dementia is a long-term neurological condition that can impact on a person's communication, memory and perception. Rosemary and I have worked alongside hundreds of people with dementia and during this time we have learned a number of important lessons.

The first is that in spite of what the newspapers and television programmes say it is possible to have a diagnosis of dementia and maintain a good quality of life with as much richness and happiness as before receiving a diagnosis.

The second lesson we have learned is that no two people will experience dementia in exactly the same way. Tom Kitwood, a wonderful sociologist and psychologist who wrote in the 1980s, said that the impact dementia has on a person will depend on a whole host of things including the level of neurological damage the dementia has caused, the individual's personality, their life history or biography and the level of social support they receive.

What is key is the importance of recognising and respecting the person. Kitwood talked about something called personhood which he described as follows:

Personhood is a standing or status that is bestowed upon one human being, by others, in the context of a relationship and social being. It implies recognition, respect and trust.[5]

In this book we have described a series of activities that you can engage in or share. If you are sharing these with a person with dementia it is important to pay attention to how this is done. We would like to suggest that there is a series of principles underpinning good dementia care that can promote personhood and these are called the RESTOR8 principles[6]. We have included an outline of these below[7].

Activating: ability-focused, meaningful activity, adapted to abilities, whether spontaneous or planned. Finding out the level of function and working within the capabilities of the individual providing as many opportunities for choice and involvement as possible.

Restoring relationship of a person to their former self and to others around them by building an image of the person through activities and roles which match the former lifestyle, individual preferences and current cognitive level of an individual through a range of therapeutic media using the biography to inform these with accurate ongoing assessment, thus providing a mutual and 'complete community'.

Developing an environment where novelty and new experiences gently challenge and stimulate individuals, probing for improved function; thus, ongoing learning experiences can take place.

Communicating an approach to activities in a way which includes an imaginative presentation ... the potential of them to be appreciated by all involved, so that all can enjoy making the ordinary extraordinary, focusing on the 'little things that matter'. This will involve an intense understanding and effective communication skills.

Enriching the environment to maximise well-being; it should aim to be stable and peaceful and offer a range of targeted, meaningful activities and 'sensory enrichments' and which foster interdependent, mutual social-supported living: access to animals, children, nature and the outdoors and the wider community where possible.

Releasing creativity within the relationships surrounding the person, which can be tapped into for the mutual support and benefit of the person with dementia, through education and understanding.

Empathising by validation and support of the emotional experience of the world lived in by the person with dementia, and how it affects those in relationship with them.

Connecting with the wider community and preventing social isolation.

R. Hurtley, RESTOR8 Principles, 2006
Email: hurtley@btinternet.com

NOTES

1. D. Weaks, H. Wilkinson, A. Houston, J. McKillop, *Perspectives on Ageing with Dementia* (York: Joseph Rowntree Foundation, 2012) p.8.
2. Rosemary Hurtley 2006.
3. Adapted from: M. Davis, E.R. Eshelman, M. Mckay, *The Relaxation and Stress Reduction Workbook* (CA. Oakland, New Harbinger, 1988).
4. Agnes Houston, 'Making things more real'. *Journal of Dementia Care* 17 6 (2009) pp.20–21.
5. Tom Kitwood, *Dementia Reconsidered* (Open University Press, 1997) p.8.
6. Rosemary Hurtley 2006.
7. J. Burton Jones, R. Hurtley, *Find the Right Care Home*, Age Concern 2008.

BIBLIOGRAPHY

Bryden C. *Dancing with Dementia* (London: Jessica Kingsley Publishers, 2005).

Goldsmith M. *Hearing the Voice of People with Dementia: Opportunities and Obstacles* (London: Jessica Kingsley, 1996).

Hurtley R. *Insight into Dementia* (Farnham: CWR, 2010).

Jewell A. *Spirituality and Personhood in Dementia* (London: Jessica Kingsley Publishers, 2011).

Killick, J. and Craig C. *Creativity and Communication in Persons with Dementia* (London: Jessica Kingsley Publishers, 2011).

Killick J. *You Are Words: Dementia Poems* (London: Hawker Publications, 1997).

Shamy E. *A Guide to the Spiritual Dimension of Care for People with Alzheimer's Disease and Related Dementia* (London: Jessica Kingsley Publishers, 2003).

Whitman L. *Telling Tales about Dementia: Experiences of Caring* (London: Jessica Kingsley Publishers, 2010).